Chinese for Beginners

BY GETAWAY GUIDES

The Best Handbook for Learning to Speak Chinese

2nd Edition

Table Of Contents

Introduction

I want to thank you and congratulate you for purchasing the book, “Chinese for Beginners: The Best Handbook for Learning to Speak Chinese”.

This book contains proven steps and strategies on how to learn the Chinese language in the fastest and easiest way. The Chinese language is the world’s most widely spoken language. Billions of people speak it as their native language, and few millions more use it as their second language. Learning it would greatly help, because chances are, you will need it for travel, business, studies, work opportunities, or even when simply dining out in that new Chinese restaurant.

Read on and learn how to speak Chinese the fastest and easiest way.

Thanks again for purchasing this book. I hope you enjoy it!

Chapter 1. Introduction to the Chinese Language

The Chinese language is actually a family of different languages or dialects. It is a family within a family. The distinction between a language and a dialect is often blurred within the Chinese language. Cantonese Chinese spoken in Hong Kong, for example, belongs to this family. Both Cantonese and Mandarin use the same group of Chinese characters, but speak very differently. Hence, a group of people versed in Cantonese can communicate in writing with people versed in Mandarin. But they couldn't one bit of what the other is saying when they speak to each other.

Mandarin Chinese

The officially recognized Chinese language is called Mandarin Chinese. It is the official language of China and Taiwan. It is also one of Singapore's and the United Nations' official languages. Mandarin Chinese is the world's top language based on the number of native speakers.

Throughout China, Mandarin Chinese is spoken in different versions, depending on the province. These are often classified as dialects. Some do consider Mandarin Chinese itself as a dialect belonging to the Chinese language family.

All of the different Chinese languages are tonal. The meaning changes depending on how it is pronounced. In Mandarin, there are 4 tones used. Others can have as much as 10 tones.

Mandarin in itself is also a group of languages. It refers both to the dialect spoken in Beijing and another spoken in China's central north region and in Inner Mongolia, which also referred to as Jin-yu or Jin.

The world refers to the Chinese official language as Mandarin, but they themselves refer to it as Huá yŭ, Guó yŭ or Pŭ tōng huà. Mainland China refers to their official Mandarin language as Pŭ tōng huà, which translates to the meaning "common language". Taiwan refers to it as Guó yŭ, which means "national language". Malaysia and Singapore call it Huá yŭ, meaning "Chinese language".

Learning Chinese

Chinese is written using their special Chinese characters. There are so many characters that represent certain words, syllables, even short phrases. This makes learning the language even more difficult. Another reason that makes the language difficult to learn is the tones. Different pronunciations give different meanings to a word. When Mandarin (the one used in the capital of Beijing) was declared as the common language, the government also simplified some of the characters. Furthermore, Romanization was also adopted. This method uses the Roman alphabet in place of the Chinese characters. This way, a student of the language does not have to learn and memorize the long list of Chinese characters just to learn how to speak it. The Roman letters represents how the Chinese words should be pronounced. There are several Romanization systems used in the study of Mandarin and the most commonly used in Pinyin.

For example, the Chinese negative word is written as 不 . A person unfamiliar with Chinese characters would have no idea what this is. And learning Chinese characters before learning to speak the language is a very long route to learning the language. To help, the Chinese character is Romanized to how it is pronounced, which is ***bù***. Thus, a person can still learn to speak the language even without having to learn the long list of Chinese characters.

Mandarin Tones

The 4 different tones in Mandarin are used to convey a clearer meaning to the words. In Chinese, several characters share the same sound. Tones set the meanings apart. The tones are:

1st tone or the high level

This tone is often denoted as the number 1 written right after the Chinese word. It can also be denoted as a short horizontal bar over the vowel. For example, the 1st tone of the word Chinese word "ma" is written as ma1 or mā. This means "mother". This is pronounced as a flat vowel sound.

2nd tone or rising

The 2nd tone is pronounced with a rising intonation on the vowel. It is denoted as the number 2 at the end of the word or with a slant line going upwards towards the right. For example, the same Chinese word "ma" in the second tone is written as "má" or ma2. The vowel "a" is pronounced with a rising intonation. This word means "hemp". See the huge difference in the meaning with just a difference in the tone.

3rd tone or falling rising

The 3rd tone is denoted as the number 3 at the end of the word or a short upward curve over the vowel. It is pronounced with a falling then rising intonation on the vowel sound. The 3rd tone of the Chinese word "ma" is written as "ma3" or "mă". It is pronounced as a prolonged vowel sound, more like "ma-a". The first "a" is pronounced in a falling intonation and the second "a" is spoken with a rising intonation. The word means "horse".

4th tone or falling

The 4th tone is the falling intonation on the vowel sound. It is denoted with a downward slant line above the vowel or the number 4 at the end of the word. For the Chinese word "ma" in the 4th tone, it is written as ma4 or "mà". This word means "scold".

These tones are most important in the Romanized method of learning Chinese. When using Chinese characters, these tones are denoted in a much different way. Often, the difference in tones totally changes the form of the written character.

Also, the tones and meanings change when it used with other words and tones. For example, the negative word ***bù***. This is in the 4th tone. But when used next to another word in the 4th tone, the negative word changes its tone into the 2nd one. It becomes "bú".

Learning the correct tones is much easier with more frequent use. As the ear becomes more acquainted with the sounds, the different tones will come naturally.

The best way to learn Chinese fast is to speak the language as often as possible. Get more opportunities to speak the language. Experts even recommend learning Chinese phrases first. This is because of the changing meanings of words related to tones and words used in a phrase. The same word can be used in several ways, with different contexts. It is still best to learn language through listening and speaking, rather than learning the grammatical rules.

Chapter 2. Chinese Pronunciation

With more than 40,000 Chinese words, beginners should not worry about trying to sound like a native on the first time they try to pronounce a Chinese syllable? Unless thoroughly exposed to the culture, no one does it perfectly on the first try. Like other language, more exposure to the culture can bridge towards eloquence in such a rich language.

Beginners can try to practice the sounds and the tones by pronouncing them out loud. Eventually the sound will be as spot on as Bruce Lee in a kung-fu movie. Hearing a native speak in ordinary speed can be intimidating at first but these people are speaking the language ever since they learn how to speak.

Each morpheme (the smallest form that possesses meaning in a language) in the Chinese language is represented by a syllable. Each syllable is composed of an initial sound and a final sound, modulated by a distinct tone. This is applicable to all Chinese syllables. These three components must be present for your Chinese pronunciation to be comprehensible.

Take the syllable "mā" which is composed of the primary sound "m" and the final sound "ā" modulated by a first tone. The parts when taken together mean "mother." If instead of first tone modulation, the third tone is used it becomes "mă" which meant "horse." This is how important tones are in pronunciation.

Pinyin

The literal meaning of pinyin is spelling a word the way the word is pronounced. This is the equivalent of phonetics in the English language. China, the big country that it is, has for many decades devised many ways to translate Chinese. In 1979, it was decided by the Chinese government that pinyin is officially the Romanization system of the Chinese language. Ever since this pronouncement by the Chinese government, different libraries and state agencies followed by assiduously changing all literature that bears other Romanization system to the Pinyin counterpart.

The following facts are the more prominent difference in how the initial Mandarin sound in each Chinese syllable:

J This consonant should be pronounced like the ketter "g" in "gelatin." The "j" is often followed by an "i." For example, "How much money?" is ***"Ji kuài qián?"*** in Chinese.

X This consonant almost always precedes an "i." This consonant sounds similar to how the "sh" is pronounced in "shop." ***Dèng Xiaopíng*** a prominent Chinese leader, used this consonant for his surname.

Z This consonant sound like "dz." The first leader of the People's Republic of China, ***Máo Zédōng*** is formerly named in important documents as Mao Tse-tung.

D, G and B Before the People's Republic of China adopted Pinyin, the sound by these consonants are Romanized respectively by the letters T, K, and P. The initial sounds of these consonants were taught in the past to be pronounced in an *aspirated* manner. (*Aspirated means having an air come out of the mouth similar to how the words "Thick", "kick" and "pick" are pronounced. As such, these letters would have been represented by* "t'," "k'," and "p'." Only aspirated letters are represented by the consonants "T," "K," and "P."

Q This letter should be pronounced like the "ch" in "chess." Unlike in English the letter Q is often followed by the letter "u", the letter Q is followed by an "i" then followed by a consonant or a vowel. ***Qīngdao,*** Chinese for beer is formerly spelled as "Tsingtao" or "ch'ing tao" in other Romanization.

Zh Unlike the consonant "j," which is often followed by a vowel to produce a more fluid sound when it is pronounced while opening the mouth, "zh" precedes vowels which makes a fluid sound while it is pronounced with mouth that is a little closed. For example: ***Zhōu Enlái,*** a renowned statesman in the history of the modern day China. His name is pronounced or read as Joe En-lye.

C This consonant sounds like how "ts" must be pronounced. Examples are the words: ***cèsuo*** (restroom) and ***cài*** (food).

Initial Sounds

In the Chinese language, consonants always comprise the initial sounds.

Chinese Letter	Sound	English Example
ch	chir	churn
sh	shir	shirt
f	faw	for
w	wuh	walk
q	chee	chapter

t	tuh	toll
p	paw	pollen
z	dzuh	“ds” in buds
d	duh	dull
l	luh	lump
h	huh	hunt
k	kuh	comment
r	ir	“er” in better
m	maw	moment
x	she	she
b	baw	bored
n	nuh	numb
g	guh	guilt
s	suh	sulk
zh	jir	germination
y	yuh	yap
c	tsuh	“ts” in nuts
j	gee	jester

The initials “-n” and “-r” are also used as a final sound in Chinese syllables.

Final Sounds

The language can boast of many consonants than there is vowel however it still has more vowels than the English language. Chinese uses six vowels: ***a, e, i, o, u,*** and ***ü***. Pronunciation of the vowels involves the mouth starting off wide while the tongue twitches off low. The last vowel ***"ü"*** is pronounced with a mouth more closed with the tongue ending high. The other vowel sounds are combination of the six primary vowels.

Chinese Vowel Sound		English Example
ang	ahng	rung
an	ahn	online
ao	ow	bow
ai	i	eye
a	ah	lot
o	aw	straw
ong	oong	too + ng
e	uh	push
ei	ay	day
en	un	run
eng	ung	sung
er	ar	are
i	ee	tea
ia	ya	gotcha
iao	yaow	meow
ie	yeh	yet
iu	yo	leo

ian	yan	cheyenne
iang	yahng	y + angst
in	een	seen
ing	eeng	going
iong	yoong	you + ng
u	oo	too
ua	wa	suave
uo	waw	war
ui	way	way
uai	why	why
üe	yweh	you + eh
uan	wan	want
un	one	one
uang	wahng	wan + ng
ü	yew	ewe
ün	yewn	you + n
üan	ywan	you + wan
ueng	wung	one + ng

Vowels are marked with tone symbols in pinyin. For two adjacent vowels the tone marks appear on the first vowel. This marks the difference between tone on the first or the final sound. The only exception to this are the vowel sounds ***ui*** and ***iu***. In both cases, the tone mark shall be made on the second vowel.

There are times when vowels are without any accompanying consonant and would often mean something informal. A good example is the word “***ai***” which means “short” (in stature.)

Chapter 3. Commonly Used Chinese Words

To start learning to speak the language, start with the vocabulary. Learn and memorize the commonly used Chinese words to get started.

Here is a comprehensive list of commonly used Chinese words.

General words

Yes ***shi***

No bú shì.

Good *hao*

Bad bù hao

Please ***qíng***

Pronouns

I ***wo***

We ***wo mén***

You (for familiar person, singular) ***niv.***

You (formal, singular) ***nin***

You (plural) ***niv mén***

They ***ta- mén***

Referring to Nationality or Foreign Language

English yi-ng yuv.

Chinese puv to-ng hùa / hàn yuv.

French ***fá yuv.***

Spanish xi- bán yá yuv.

German dé yuv.

Referring to People

Husband zhàng fu-.

Wife qi- ziv.

Father ***ba- ba***

Mother ***ma- ma***

Son ***ér zi***

Daughter ***nüv er***

Friend péng youv.

Numbers

Zero ***líng***

One yi-.

Two ***èr***

Three san-.

Four sì

Five wuv.

Six lìu

Seven ***qi-.***

Eight ***ba-.***

Nine jiuv.

Ten ***shí***

Eleven shí yi-.

Twelve shí èr

Thirteen shí san-.

Fourteen shí sì

Fifteen shí wuv.

Sixteen shí liù

Seventeen shí qi-.

Eighteen shí bav.

Nineteen shí jiuv.

Twenty ***èr shí***

Twenty-one èr shí yi-.

Twenty-two èr shí èr

Thirty san- shí

Forty sì shí

Fifty wuv shí

Sixty liù shí

Seventy qi- shí

Eighty ba- shí

Ninety jiuv shí

One hundred yì baiv.

One hundred one ***yì baiv yì***

One thousand ***yì qianv.***

One million yì baiv wàn

Ordinal Numbers

First **dì yĩ**

Second **dì èr**

Third **dì sān**

Fourth **dì sì**

Fifth **dì wu**

Sixth **dì liù**

Seventh **dì qĩ**

Eighth **dì bā**

Ninth **dì jiu**

Tenth **dì shí**

Food

Breakfast zaov can-.

Lunch wuv can-.

Dinner wanv can-.

Kosher yóu tài hé fav shí wù

Vegetarian sù shí zhev.

Beverage **yinv liào**

Tea **chá**

Water **shuiv.**

Wine **jiuv.**

Beer pí jiuv.

Coffee ka- fei-.

Juice guov zhi-.

Bread miàn bao-.

Pepper hú jiao-.

Salt ***yán***

Meat ***roù***

Pork zhu- roù

Beef niú roù

Poultry jia- qinv.

Fish ***yú***

Fruit shuiv guov.

Vegetable ***cài***

Potato mav líng shuv.

Dessert tián pinv.

Salad ***sa- là***

Ice cream bing- qi- lín / xuev gào

Days

Day Rì / tian-.

Week xing- qi-.

Year ***nián.***

Monday xing- qi- yi-.

Tuesday xing- qi- èr

Wednesday xing- qi- san-.

Thursday xing- qi- sì

Friday xing- qi- wuv.

Saturday xing- qi- liù

Sunday xing- qi- rì / xing- qi- tiàn

Months of the year

Month ***yùe.***

January ***yi- yùe***

February ***èr yùe***

March ***san- yùe***

April ***sì yùe***

May wuv yùe

June ***liù yùe***

July ***qì yùe***

August ***bà yùe***

September ***jiuv yùe***

October ***shí yùe***

November shí yi- yùe

December ***shí èr yùe***

Seasons and Time

Summer ***xià.***

Spring ***chun-.***

Winter ***dòng.***

Autumn/Fall ***qiu-.***

Yesterday ***zúo tian-.***

Today	jin- tian-.
Tomorrow	míng tian-.
What time is it?	jí dianv zhòng le?
Three-fifteen (3:15)	san- dianv shí wuv fen-.
Quarter past three (3:15)	***san- dianv yí kè***
Seven-thirteen (7:13)	qi- dianv shí san- fen-.
Eleven-thirty (11:30)	shí yi- dianv san- shí fen-.
Half past eleven (11:30)	***shí yi- dianv bàn***
One forty-five (1:45)	yi- dianv sì shí wuv fen-.
Quarter till two (1:45)	yi- dianv sì shí wuv fen-.

Chapter 4. Greeting and Conversing

Greetings in Chinese are often accompanied with a light handshake. The hand is held a bit longer while greetings are exchanged. Sometimes a hand shake is held for as long as 10 seconds. Some prefer to greet with a bow instead of a hand shake. When greeting, it is better to wait for the Chinese to make the first move to see if they prefer a hand shake or a bow.

The most common greeting in Chinese, it translates as "***nǐ hǎo***". It literally translates to "You good, but is most often regarded as the generic "hi" and "hello". It can be used loosely in any situation, as one would with Hi and hello.

In Chinese, greetings differ when it is spoken formally or informally. For example, when saying "Good morning" in a formal setting, one would say "***zǎoshàng hǎo***". When saying the same greeting to someone more familiar, one can just say "***nǐ zǎo***" or simply "***zǎo***". "Good afternoon" is "***xiàwǔ hǎo***" and "Good evening" is "***wǎnshàng hǎo***".

Another way of conversing is asking about the other person, such as "How are you?" and "How is it going?" These often follow the standard greetings. In Chinese, these are spoken as:

"***nǐ hǎoma?***" (How are you?)

Notice that part of that phrase is "***nǐ hǎo***", which means Hi or Hello. With the addition of the syllable –ma, the meaning changes. This is an example of Chinese word and phrase that totally changes in meaning when tones and characters are added.

Other phrases used to ask about the other person are:

How is it going? ***nǐ zěnmeyàng?***

How's it going lately? ***zuìjìn zěnmeyàng?***

How are you lately? ***zuìjìn hǎoma?***

Responses also vary to the question "How are you?" Formal polite responses would be:

I'm doing great, thank you. ***wǒ hěnhǎo, xièxie.***

I'm not doing well. ***wǒ bútàihǎo.***

Responses in informal, more familiar way would be:

So-so. *mǎmǎhūhū.*

This is only to be used among close friends. This phrase literally translates to "Horse Horse Tiger Tiger". This response is treated as the counterpart for the English "So-so" response only among very close friends. Other responses that can be used in informal settings include:

I'm okay. ***háixíng.***

I'm fine. ***tǐnghǎode.***

Making Introductions

Compared to to other cultures, the Chinese people can across as being more formal. However, it is not impolite at all to start a conversation with them and introduce one's self, as long as it is done with the right manner. It does not have to be lengthy or complicated. A few phrases are often enough.

To ask for person's name:

nǐ jiào shénme míngzi? What is your name?

nín guì xìng? What is your last name?

These are formal methods of making introductions.

wǒ jiào Anna My name is Anna.

wǒ xìng Smith. My surname is Smith.)

Sharing Personal Information

Making small talk often involves sharing some personal information such as hobbies, work or place of origin. A few handy phrases to ask someone or answer someone's question are the following:

- What country are you from? (***nǐ cóng nǎge guójiā lái?***) or Where are you from? (***nǐ cóng nǎr lái?***)
- I am from France. ***wǒ cóng fǎguó lái.***
- I am from Canada. **wǒ cóng jiānádà lái.**

I am from the United States. ***wǒ cóng měiguó lái.***

I am from Mexico. ***wǒ cóng mòxīgē lái.***

I am from the United Kingdom. ***wǒ cóng yīngguó lái.***

I am from Spain. ***wǒ cóng xībānyá lái.***

I am from Japan. ***wǒ cóng rìběn lái.***

- What city are you from? ***nǐ cóng nǎge chéngshì lái?***

I am from Los Angeles. ***wǒ cóng xiàn lái.***

I am from Chicago. wǒ cóng zhījiāgē lái.

I am from New York. ***wǒ cóng niǔyuē lái.***

I am from Paris. ***wǒ cóng bālí lái.***

I am from Madrid. ***wǒ cóng mǎdélǐ lái.***

I am from Tokyo. wǒ cóng dōngjīng lái.

- What do you do? nǐ shì zuò shénme de?

I am here on a study- abroad program. ***wǒ zài zhèr liúxué.***

I am here to study Chinese. ***wǒ zài zhèr xué zhōngwén.***

I am a student. ***wǒ shì xuéshēng.***

I'm a doctor. ***wǒ shì yīshēng***.

Where are you going? ***niv qù na liv?***

- Do you have a girlfriend? ***nǐ yǒu nǚpéngyou ma?***
- Do you have a boyfriend? ***nǐ yǒu nánpéngyou ma?***
- Are you married? ***nǐ jiēhūnle ma?***

- Where do you live? ***niv zhù zài na liv?***
- Do you have any children? ***nǐ yǒu háizi ma?***

No, I don't have any children. ***wǒ méiyǒu háizi.***

When having conversations, be aware that some topics are off limits. Some topics may appear as too personal, such as topics about salaries and marital affairs. There are also very sensitive topics that should always be avoided. These are about Tibet and Taiwan, which have a long, complex history that can ruffle more than a few feathers. It is easy to offend a lot of people with these topics.

Personal Interests

Having conversations may also include personal interests aside from sharing personal information.

- How do you have fun? ***nǐ xǐhuān wán shénme?***

I don't watch television. ***wǒ bú kàn diànshì***.

I like going to the movies. ***wǒ xǐhuān kàn diànyǐng***.

I like to go dancing. ***wǒ xǐhuān qù tiàowǔ***.

- Do you play any sports? nǐ xǐhuān shénme yùndòng ma?
- I am a big sports fan. ***wǒ shì yí gè yùndòng mí.***
- I play soccer. ***wǒ tī zúqiú***.

I like playing golf. ***wǒ dǎ gāoěrfū qiú.***

- What type of food excites you? ***nǐ xǐhuān chī shénmeyàng de fàn?***
- This is my favorite restaurant. **zhè shì wǒ zuì xǐhuān de fànguǎn**.

Compliments

Compliments are important in the Chinese culture, here are good examples of phrases that can be used to dispense compliments:

Awesome! ***bàng jí le!***

Congratulations! ***nǐ zuò de hěn hǎo!***

You've done an exceptional job! ***nǐ zuò de hěn chū sè!***

You are truly remarkable! ***nǐ zhēn liǎo bù qǐ!***

You are great! ***nǐ tài bàng le!***

Quite a surprise! zhēn méi xiǎng dàn!

You are a wonderful man! ***nǐ zhēn shì gè hǎo rén!***

What a lovely place! zhè lǐ zhēn piāo liàng!

You are the greatest in our firm. nǐ shì wǒ mén gōng sī zuì yōu xiù de yuán gōng

Other Polite Phrases

Politeness can go a long way, especially when interacting with people from another culture. Here are a few phrases that can be of use:

Thank you ***xìe xìe***

Thank you very much fei- cháng gàn xìe / henv gàn xìe

You're welcome. ***bu yong xie***

Excuse me. qivng ràng, dui bu qi

Goodbye

Ending a meeting is usually with a "Goodbye", which is ***zàijiàn*** in Chinese. There are also other forms of saying goodbye, such as ***mànzǒu***, which means "Take care". It literally translates to "Walk carefully", but is generally accepted as "Take care". ***Mànzǒu*** is an informal phrase. The formal form of this phrase is "**bǎozhòng**".

Other ways of saying "Goodbye" after a conversation include:

Good luck!	*zhù nǐ hǎoyùn!*
See you tomorrow.	***míngtiān jiàn***.
See you next week.	***xiàge xīngqījiàn***.
See you soon.	***huítóu jiàn***.
Talk to you soon.	***gǎitiān zàiliáo***.

These are simple yet very effective conversation starters. Small talk helps in gaining friends, as well as in practicing Speaking Chinese. With more practice, the right tones and a deeper understanding of the language will eventually come naturally.

Chapter 5. Chinese For Business Settings

In the Chinese culture, job hierarchy is important. The kind of work they do are serious matters that must not at all be taken too lightly. They are also excellent topics for conversations. A good conversation starter is to ask someone about their ***gōngzuò*** (work). The question, ***"Ni zuò shénme gōngzuò?"*** ("What is your line of work?) is a good way to begin. A good follow-up to this question is trying to guess their job with: ***"Ni shì kuàijì ma?"*** (Do you happen to be an accountant?).

The ***dānwèi*** (work unit) is an important aspect in the life of many Chinese people. The term refers to the workplace which can be in anywhere in China. The ***dānwèi*** is the unit responsible for guiding people in their responsibilities in the workplace. The group will look after their member's performance and every missteps they take while in the workplace.

It should not come as a surprise when they ask people over the phone, **"*Ni nar?*"** (Where are you from?) to know what ***dānwèi*** they belong to. During the administration of the founder of the People's Republic of China (who also happens to be the figure head of the Chinese Communist Party), people were given jobs right after finishing high school. The location of job assignment were more important than or a determinant of the viability of marriage.

The ***dānwèi*** provides housing for their employees and enforces rules and promulgations by the government like the one-child-per-family policy. Permission from the unit is necessary for marriage, child-bearing. Government benefits are channeled through the unit.

Chinese employees could have been assigned to the northern provinces of China while their fiancées could have been sent to the southern cities. If such was the case, couples can only see their other half only once each year: every Chinese New Year.

Addressing People

For Western countries such as the United States of America, having a lot of ***lao péngyou*** (old friends) are normal. In China or any of their neighboring countries, it is important to address the people in the manner they are accustomed to be addressed in order to start a relationship in the right foot.

If people just knew each other, it is necessary to avoid appearing too presumptuous or too friendly. It takes some time before strangers can be less formal towards each other.

For professional and business events, it is always a safe start to greet people by addressing them by their last name before their title. A good example would be: ***Wái Xiàozhang*** (President [of a school or university] Wai) or ***Jīng Zhuguan*** (CEO Jing). Here are some other examples of occupational titles:

Occupations

The following are the Chinese translations of the occupations that can be mentioned in the course of your conversations:

Teacher	***laoshī***
Professor	***jiàoshòu***
Editor	***biānjí***
Lawyer	***lǐshī***
Doctor	***yīshēng***
Nurse	***hùshì***

Actor ***yanyuán***

CEO *zhuguan*

Accountant ***kuàijì***

Pilot fēixíngyuán

Flight Attendant ***chéngwùyuán***

Telephone Operator ***jiēxiànyuán***

Receptionist qiántái fúwùyuán

Plumber shuinuangōng

Electrician ***diàngōng***

Train Conductor ***lièchēyuán***

Customs Agent ***haiguān guānyuán***

Mail Carrier ***yóudìyuán***

Tailor ***cáifeng***

Housekeeper kèfáng fúwùyuán

Bank Teller ***chūnàyuán***

Department Head ***bùzhang***

Assistant Director ***fùzhurèn***

Manager ***jīngli***

Aside from the above occupation titles, these are useful job-related expressions that can come in handy:

Employee ***gùyuán***

Employer ***gùzhu***

Part-time work ***bàn rì gōngzuò***

Full-time work **quán rì gō**

Unemployed **shīyè**

Interview **miànshì**

The information about a person's title isn't always available so it is also safe to address someone by announcing the person's last name and then follow it up by either: ***Xiānshēng*** (Mr.) or ***Xiaojie*** (Miss).

Requests and Appointments

Chinese people are hospitable people, these key phrases when requesting something or setting an appointment may come in handy:

Can I ask you a little favor?	gēn nín shāng liàng gè shìr?
Could I borrow a hundred yuan?	néng bù néng jiè wǒ yī bǎi kuài qián?
Mr. Tang, can you please assist me with this document?	xiǎo táng, néng bù néng bāng wǒ bǎ zhè fèn wén jiàn fù yìn yī xià?
Let's talk about we our plans will be tomorrow.	wǒ mén shāng liàng yī xià míng tiān gàn shá ba.
We will be riding the train to Guangzhou first then we will be flying to Hong Kong.	wǒ mén xiān zuò huǒ chē dào guǎng zhōu , rán hòu huàn fēi jī dào xiāng gang.
How about this thought?	nǐ kàn zhè yàng xíng bù xíng?
It's too late. Why don't we go tomorrow?	tài wǎn le. míng tiān zài qù rú hé?
Fine, you have my word.	Hǎo, yī yán wéi ding.
Okay, you choose.	Xíng, tīng nǐ de.

Then it's decided.	jiù zhè yàng ba.
Let's schedule it on Sunday.	nà jiù xīng qī tiān ba.
As you want.	jiù àn nín de yì sī bàn
I will come a minute after you go in first.	nǐ xiān qù wǒ mǎ shàng jiù lái.
Well that's settled and you should keep your promise.	nà jiù zhè me dìng le, kě bié fǎn huǐ a.

Chapter 6. Directions

Basic Directions

Tourists often go to Chinese-speaking countries because of their rich and unique culture. It can be quite an adventure especially that not a lot of people in this country know English. Asking directions is very important to avoid making mistakes in places that may be unfamiliar. Making sense of the instructions given is important. There's no use knowing how to ask for directions if the instructions narrated by the locals are all gibberish.

Chinese-speaking countries are hospitable people so knowing how to ask for directions can be a piece of cake. In order to successfully ask for help, tourists can ask: ***máfan nín, wǒ kěyǐ gēn nín wènlù ma?*** (Excuse me, may I ask you some instructions about directions?). It is important to pay attention to what these people are saying in order to reach the desired destination.

Nearby	***fùjìn***
Far	***yuǎn***
Next to	**pángbiān**
In front of	***qiánmiàn***
Close	***jìn***
Behind	***hòumiàn***
North	***běi***
East	***dōng***
West	***xī***

South ***nán***

Right ***yòu***

Left ***zuǒ***

Turn right ***wàng yòu guǎi***

Turn left ***wàng zuǒ guǎi***

Around the block ***zài lù kǒu***

Keep going straight ***yìzhízǒu***

At the corner ***zài guǎi jiǎo***

Public Places

Passport ***hù zhào***

Ticket ***piao***

Arrival ***rù jìng***

Departure ***chu- jìng***

Parking tíng che- changv.

Bus gong- gòng qì che- / gong- che-.

Bus Station gong- gòng qì che- zhàn / gong- che- zhàn

Airport fei- ji- changv.

Train huov che-.

Train Station ***huov che- zhàn***

Underground/Subway ***dì tiev.***

Underground Station ***dì tiev zhàn***

Car rental	chu- zu- qì chè zhang-.
Hotel	lü' guanv.
Reservation	***yù lang***
Room	***kè lang***
No vacancies	kè manv / méi youv kong- lang
Post office	***yóu jú***
Tourist information	***liuv yóu wèn xún chù***
Bank	yín lang
Museum	bó wú guanv.
Shop/Store	***diàn***
Police station	***jingv chá jú***
Hospital	***yi- yuàn***
Church	jiào lang
School	xúe xiáo
Restaurant	***jiuv lóu***
Chemist/Pharmacy	***yào lang***
Swimming pool	yóu yongv chí
Restroom	xiv shouv jian-.
Square	fang-, guang chang
Street	***jie-.***
Tower	***tav.***
Bridge	***qiáo***
Hill	shan- / qiu-.

Valley	shan- guv.
Mountain	***shan-.***
Lake	***hú***
River	***hé***
Ocean	haiv, yang

Other Helpful Phrases

Aside from the directions above, here are some questions that can come in handy when in need of directions or instructions from the locals.

Would you please give us instructions how?	nǐ kěyǐ gàosù wǒmen zěnme qǜa ma?
How far is the train station from the hotel?	cóng huǒchēzhàn dào lǚguǎn yǒu duōyuǎn?
Should I take a bus?	wǒ yīnggāi zuò chē ma?
Could you speak slower?	qǐng nín shuō màn yì diǎn, hǎoma?
Go right and then look for the first street to your left.	wàng yòu guǎi* zài nǐ zuǒbiān de dìyītiáo jiē
	zuìjìn de yínháng zài nǎlǐ/nǎr?
Could you please say that again?	qǐng nín zài shuō yí cì, hǎoma?
What is the number of the bus?	zuò jǐlù chē?
Do you have an idea how to get there?	nǐ zhīdào zěnme qǜ nàlǐ /nǎr ma?

*Locals tend to use the words **zhuǎn** and **guǎi** interchangeable for "turn."

Chapter 7. Dining

Chinese Food

There are a lot of things to learn about Chinese food. It is not uncommon for people to find themselves as a guest in a Chinese friend's abode or even be the guest of honor in a banquet thrown by their company in a restaurant in Beijing.

Chinese people take their time with food very seriously and this should be taken into account whenever people rub elbows with them. There are certain words and phrases that will come in handy whenever tourists gets either hungry or thirsty, go to the grocery or convenience store to buy food and order food from the restaurant.

Making a good impression is key in being a wonderful guest or a well-loved host. These impressions tend to last a long time and can be used to gauge how well people conduct themselves in the restaurant as much as they do in the workplace. More often than not, people only have one shot at doing this right.

The Chinese cuisine is famous not only in the neighboring countries but also in the Western world. People have always filled the tables of Chinese restaurants and flocked the China town for savory and delectable Chinese delicacies. The fanfare when it comes to the great Chinese dishes does not begin and end with just the sweet and sour pork, chop suey and the chow mien, and the very famous Chinese dim sum.

Some say that you will know a lot about a person by his food. True enough, eating Chinese food and exploring Chinese eating decorum is a good way to be immersed with the rich Chinese culture. This is not even about merely impressing a date to how much a person knows about the culture but really getting to know China in its purest and most delicious form.

All about the Food

Chinese people take pride in their cuisine. For people who have yet to be acquainted with the tasty ***fàn*** (food), they can go to a nice Chinese restaurant downtown to ***chī*** (eat)

The word ***fàn*** is very prominent in China whenever people are talking about their meals. For example, a typical meal plan for the day consists of:

Breakfast (Morning meal) ***zaofàn***

Lunch (Second meal) ***wufàn***

Dinner (Evening meal) ***wanfàn***

The Chinese cuisine is very important to the people such that it has been part of their custom that instead of greeting each other with ***"Ni hao ma?"*** (How are you?), they ask each other ***"Ni chīfàn le méiyou?"*** ("Have you eaten?")

The word ***Fàn*** does not only connote food in China. Its literal meaning is any kind of starch-based or grain food staple. ***Mifan*** (Rice) is always part of the Chinese dining experience as Chinese culture.

In fact rice has many variations:

Boiled white rice ***bái mifàn***

Steamed buns ***bāozi***

Fried Rice ***chao fàn***

Noodles ***miàntiáo***

Dumplings ***jiaozi***

Having many types of ***fàn*** shows how important rice-based foods are to the Chinese culture.

Other Food

Meat ***ròu***

Chicken ***jīròu***

Lamb ***yángròu***

Beef ***niúròu***

Fish ***yú***

Shrimp ***xiā***

Squid ***yóuyú***

Lobster ***lóngxiā***

Crab ***pángxiè***

Fruit ***Shuiguo***

Orange ***júzi***

Apples ***píngguo***

Inviting People to Eat

In a regular setting, people can express their hunger by saying ***wo hen è*** (I'm starving) and wait until a good friend will invite them for lunch or a quick food break. For people who want to say they are thirsty they can just say ***wode kou hen ke*** (literal: my mouth is salivating) until people offers them with different varieties of drinks.

Often, people don't have to even say those phrases as they will offer you food on the onset. In Chinese custom, practicing the rules of hospitality is important. This includes the offer of food and drinks to guests the moment the guest is admitted inside the household.

There are subtler ways for people to send the idea that they are hungry without being too forward or blatant. They can say:

Are you hungry? ***Ni è ma?*** (formal)

Ni è bú è? (informal)

I bet you have yet to have dinner. ***Ni hái méi chī wanfàn ba.***

Chinese people attend to the needs of others first so it us customary to check to see whether the other persons in the room are hungry. This sensibility of being very considerate of others earns the respect of anyone who has grown in the Chinese culture. This sets a welcome atmosphere that gives the person who asked those questions, the chance to announce that he badly wants some Chinese food.

There is another way to do this. A person can substitute ***wo*** (I) for ***ni*** (you). The word ***ba*** at the end of any statement is an accessory word that means "I bet." A good example is: ***Ni hái méi chī wanfàn ba*** (I bet you have yet to have dinner.) The phrase can also mean "let's," as it is in ***Women qù chīfàn ba*** (Let's eat dinner). The intonation of how the words are pronounced can soften the sound for it to appear as a respectful request or a louder enunciation if it a command.

Acquaintances can invite people for dinner by asking: ***Ni yào chī fàn háishì yào chī miàn?*** (Do you want to have noodles or rice?) It is important to remember that this question is a mere formality because Chinese hospitality dictates that the host will offer you not just rice or noodles which is their basic staple before they serve the ***cài*** which are the various viands that complements either the rice or the noodles.

When people are being offered with wine they can respond with ***Ni xiān hē jiu*** (Drink wine first). It will be better however if the phrase ***Ni xiān hē jiu ba*** (Why not have some wine?) is used to invite the host to drink wine with you.

A Chinese homemaker would often say to their children that they can eat "anything that has legs but not a table and anything that has wings but not an airplane."

Chinese cuisine has been the envy of many kitchens in the world. With not a lot to spare, the Chinese population is thought how to make no waste of even the tiniest morsel of all sources of food (animal, fruits and vegetables). Chinese households learned to be creative about the amazing dishes they are able to prepare. Chinese history has seen many years of food shortage and their people learned to make do with what they have. To these people, necessity is indeed the mother of invention.

Sitting Down for Chinese Food

In a restaurant, people may often wonder which utensils should be used to eat the meal served to them. If this is the case, people can ask for what they are used to: fork and knife. Most of the Chinese restaurants have this pair of utensils. Modern Chinese people has learned to use fork and knife but many still use chopsticks.

Utensils and Eating Accoutrements

Spoon tiáogēng

Fork ***chāzi***

Knife ***dāozi***

Napkin cānjīnzhi

Plate ***pánzi***

Bowl ***wan***

Cup bēizi

Toothpick ***yáqiān***

Chinese food comes in different varieties which can be eaten three times a day and people can still anticipate for a different dish. People can consume Chinese food on a daily basis but there will be a time when their palette will miss the good old American food like a huge serving of hamburger and a palatable stack of fries.

Ever since China opened its doors to the world, their cities are not complete with the likes of Mc Donalds', or Burger King. Pizza parlors are also present in different provinces even those that is least expected to have one.

Western Food

Fried Chicken ***zhá jī***

Hamburger ***hànbaobāo***

Hot dog ***règou***

Pizza bisā bing

French fries ***zhá shutiáo***

Spaghetti yìdàlì shì miàntiáo

Onion Rings zhá yángcōng quān

Potato	***káo tudòu***
Mashed Potatoes	***tudòuní***
Salad Bar	shālā zìzhùgui
Salad Dressing	***shālā jiàng***
Pork Chops	***zhū pái***
Lamb Chops	***yáng pái***
Sandwich	***sānmíngzhì***
Beverages	
Mineral water	***kuāngquánshui***
Milk	***niúnai***
Tea	***chá***
Soda	***kelè***
Fruit juice	***guozhī***
Lemonade	níngmén qìshui
Wine list	***jiudān***
Beer	***píjiu***
Dry red wine	gān hóng pŪtáojiu
Coffee	***kāfēi***

Proper Table Etiquette

In Chinese homes, it is imperative that guests bring a small gift as a sign of respect to the host after receiving a cordial invitation to his home. Before taking a drink, guests must offer a toast to the other people sitting in the table; otherwise, this is considered as being rude.

Slurping when eating the soup or even burping during or after the meal is not considered as disrespectful. This is normal even in formal events and family gathering. The guests are expected to be polite all throughout the meal. It is considered respectful to always try to serve others the food on the table to someone else before getting some for yourself. This is especially true when in large formal dinners. Failing to at least attempting to do any of these can be seen as risqué, rude and arrogant.

Key Phrases at the Table

There are some phrases that people can use in attempting to impress the host with newly-learned Chinese.

Màn chī or ***màn màn chī!*** (Bon appetite!) When translated literally, the phrase means "Eat slowly," but informally it is loosely translated to mean, "Take your time and enjoy your food!"

Here are other phrases that can be used:

Have some more!	***Duō chī yidiar ba!***
I'll help myself.	***Zìji lái.***
I'm stuffed.	***Wo chībao le.***
Bottoms up!	***Gānbēi!***

Whenever someone serves another person food out of courtesy, it is customary that the person must always try to pretend protest while saying **zìji lái** (I'll help myself.) This is important so as not to embarrass the person who served you some food. Also it sends a message that it is not necessary for them to serve you food like helpers.

They will still insist so in the end, the guest must permit the person to follow etiquette by letting them be served with equal portions especially made for guests.

Just like in regular restaurants or houses in the Western culture, using a **yáqiān** (*toothpick*) should be done with a covered mouth. Flashing the teeth while using toothpick is disrespectful and considered as one of the worse dining faux pas in the Chinese culture.

More about Chinese Cuisine

China is a big country. It even has as many dialects as there are provinces. Each province has its own different brand of cuisine. They are usually dependent on the climate or the amount of vegetation in the area.

Each specialties are different unique in each of the provinces. The cooking style, presentations and prominent ingredients factor in this. Some province specializes on spicy food while others prefer more bland delicacies. It is better to try a lot of the different foods to discover a new brand of taste present in the variety of cuisine.

The Northern provinces are known for their protein-rich dishes. Beijing restaurants serve plenty of lamb, beef and duck (like the famous Peking duck.) These provinces garnish their food with garlic, scallions and meat for added taste however the northern style is known for producing bland is food due to the lack of seasoning and excessive condiments unlike southern cooking which are generally sweeter, spicier and saltier.

Eastern cuisine is represented by Shanghai and neighbor Zhejiang and Jiangsu. These provinces are closer to the sea and there are also plenty of lakes scattered in the three provinces. Eastern cooking became famous for the variety of seafood they serve in their dishes. Aside from all the seafood, they garnish their dishes with fresh leafy vegetables and different varieties of bamboo.

Sugar and soy sauce are prominent in Eastern Chinese cooking. The rich sweet and salty dishes are well-loved by many tourists.

Western Chinese cuisine is prominent in the provinces of Hunan and Sichuan. In the United States, Western Chinese cooking is more prominent. This part of China is usually humid and hot, salt and hot peppers are adequately produced than in any other province. The food are a lot spicier in this part of China. (Trivia: Mao Zedong along with other famous Chinese revolutionaries came from West China.)

Southern Chinese cuisine started in Guangdong (historically known as Canton). Fujian island and Taiwan. Since these provinces are next to the sea, Southern Chinese cuisine has large amounts of seafood figured in their dishes. Fresh fruits and green leafy vegetable are also used as primary ingredients in their menu. The famous ***dim sum*** came from Guangdong which is pronounced as ***dian xīn*** by most people from the province.

Eating Out

It is important to know how to ask for familiar cutleries and how to call these items fancifully laid out on the table. The expectations are the same whether in the informal setting of a friend's place or the more formal setting of a fancy Chinese restaurant.

When you need assistance in procuring something needed, one can politely request by uttering ***Qing ni gei wo...*** (Would you mind getting me a ...) An alternative phrase that can be used is ***Máfan ni gei wo...*** (May I trouble you to please get me a...)

Here is a list of the items that people will be encountering when eating outside:

A bowl *yíge wan*

A plate *yíge pánzi*

A glass *yíge bēizi*

A spoon yíge tiáogēng

A knife yíge dāozi

A fork ***yíge chāzi***

A napkin yì zhāng cānjīn

A toothpick **yì gēn yáqiān**

A wet towel yíge shī máojīn

A hot towel *yíge rè máojīn*

A pair of chopsticks ***yì shuāng kuàizi***

Placing an Order

Whether people prefer meat ***háishì*** (or) fish, there are certainly a lot to choose from the Chinese menu. The alternative interrogative structure for questions can be more fluid by using the term ***háishì*** (or). People can use the word "or" in two affirmative statements like for example: the package will arrive either later or tomorrow morning. If this is the case, instead of ***háishì***, the term ***huò*** or ***huò zhe*** should be used.

The servers don't expect to hear perfect Chinese when they are requested to do something. It is usually fool-proof to use the word ***ge*** before mentioning the noun or object that is required. This count word modifies the noun it precedes and specifies the number of object being mentioned. ***Ge*** is often used but some people uses ***zhè*** (this) or ***nà*** (that). The Chinese language utilizes many measure words. The most common among these measure words is ***ge***.

As obvious in the above list, the article "a" has a Chinese equivalent in ***yī*** which means number 1 in Chinese. The measure word is always between the article ***yī*** and the particular noun being modified. For example, chopsticks are always used in pairs, the numerical modifier is ***shuāng*** which means pair. Another example is for napkin, the word ***zhāng*** is used as is in any object that has a flat surface like, a blanket, map or even the floor. For anything that resembles a thin stick like a thread, a rope or a blade of grass, the measuring word used is always ***gēn.***

Finding the restrooms

It is not uncommon for people to be in need of a restroom especially while dining in a restaurant. Some people might just want to freshen up or at least take a leak before doing business in the restaurant. For a crowded restaurant, it can be difficult and confusing to find the restroom. The need may even arise especially in a formal occasion that offers a 10-course feast in a high-class Beijing restaurant and while downing several glasses of ***máotái***, the tautest Chinese cocktail.

The Chinese restaurants might have Chinese characters marking key areas like a wash area. If this is the case, diners can ask the servers: ***"Nali keyi xi shou?"*** (Where can I wash my hands?)

The easy way out is to ask the attendant or the server: ***"Cèsuo zài nar?"*** (Where's the restroom?) in mainland China or say ***"Cèsuonzài nali"*** *(tsuh swaw dzye nah lee)* in Taiwan or other Southern province.

Toilet paper is not always available in public restrooms. It is important to bring some toilet paper just in case it will be needed. Tourists make it a point to take some toilet paper before they leave their hotel rooms.

Usually bathroom doors are marked with self-explanatory pictures but in case no illustrated markings are available, the pīnyīn for male is ***nán*** and female is ***nh*** followed by the word ***cèsuo.*** It is not that hard to distinguish which especially with the pīnyīn markings.

It is not unusual to come across the word ***cèsuo*** in graffiti which is often considered as ***cèsuo wénxué*** (bathroom literature).

Paying the Bill

Sampling every possible combinations of the Chinese cuisine will eventually lead down to this: paying the bill.

To go *fēnkāi suàn*

To pay the bill ***jiézhàng***

It's on me. ***Wo qing kè.***

The check, please. ***Qing jiézhàng.***

The bill is incorrect. ***Zhàngdān you cuò.***

Please give me the receipt. ***Qing kāi shōujù.***

The tip is included. ***Bāokuò fúwùfèi.***

May I use a credit card? *Wo keyi yòng xìnyòng ka ma?*

Other Handy Phrases

Where else to learn and practice speaking Chinese but in Chinese restaurants? Here are a few phrases that can be of great use when dining:

Please bring the bill. ***qingv jíe zhàng.***

Are you ready to order? ***Kěyǐ diǎn cài le ma?***

Yes, we are ready to order. ***Wǒmen yào diǎn cài.***

Please bring us some (name of food) ***Qǐng zài gěi wǒmen ...***

This is not what I ordered. ***Zhè búshì wǒ diǎn de.***

That is for me. ***Shì wǒde.***

Chapter 8. Talking Chinese on the Phone

At the advent of today's technology, there are multiple ways to communicate to families, friends or work-related personnel. Most businesses usually prefer electronic mail than phone calls because of documentation purposes, while personal and more urgent matters are discussed in phone calls.

A tight-knit family culture of the Chinese gives importance on ***shēngyīn*** (voice) from the person on the other end. Huge matters like company mergers or opening a new division can't just be handled by series of e-mails sent by division heads to each other. Most of these correspondences require voice calls.

Knowing how to handle phone calls is an important skill when dealing with Chinese businessmen compared to merely being able to use internet chat for communication. The skill of being able to converse in a different language takes time and effort which is the reason that Chinese businessmen are impressed with non-Chinese who are able to learn and speak their language.

In order to make a successful phone conversation, it is important to know the basics of using the ***diànhuà*** (telephone). First, it is important to note down the ***dìqū hàoma*** (area code) which will be ***bō*** (dialed) first. This is the crucial first step to make a call to China or to any Chinese businessman for that matter.

Using a telephone

Experience is certainly the best teacher. Before making a phone call, people should have a prepared spiel that must be enunciated clearly. Being familiar with simple and common Chinese words and phrases is definitely a big help.

In order to identify which one is being used here are the different kinds of phones being used these days:

Cell phone ***shoujī***

Cordless phone ***wúxiàn diànhuà***

Public telephone ***gōngyòng diànhuà***

Sometimes the area code is not available. In such cases, the assistance of a ***jiēxiànyuán*** (operator) is needed especially when making an important ***guójì diànhuà*** (international phone calls) or when looking for the ***diànhuà hàoma*** (telephone number) of a company or hotel.

It is rare that the assistance of a ***jiēxiànyuán*** is needed in making a ***benshì diànhuà*** (local call) although sometimes you might need them when making a ***chángtú diànhuà*** (long-distance call).

Everything else is easy to figure out except making a ***duìfāng fùfèi diànhuà*** (collect call).

Here is a list of keywords that will definitely come in handy when making a phone call:

To make a phone call ***da diànhuà***

To look a number up in a phone book ***chá diànhuà hàomabù***

Telephone number ***diànhuà hàoma***

Phone card ***diànhuàka***

Some people requires assurance from an operator before actually making an overseas call. Here are is a list of questions that can be useful:

How can I make a phone call? ***zenme da diànhuà?***

Where can I place a call? ***zài nar kéyi da diànhuà?***

How much does a local phone call cost? ***benshì diànhuà shōufèi duōshao qián?***

Using a Mobile Phone

A lot of people in the world doesn't have a telephone wired to their homes. The homes in mainland China are not any different especially in Hong Kong, Singapore and Thailand.

In progressive cities around the world, millions of people already own their own ***shoujī*** (cell phone.) People can't leave their houses without it tucked in their pockets or held in their own hand. It is now common to see people holding their phone closely to their ***zuibā*** (mouth) talking to friends or co-workers. Cell phone's portable nature has made it the choice mode of communication in this technology-savvy world.

Western producers of cell phones tried to penetrate the Chinese market but China-based brands such as Ningbo Bird and TCL are well-accepted my many users in different households.

Here are some words that are useful when referring to the use of a mobile phone:

Beep ***hū***

Beeper ***hūjī***

Beeper number ***hūjī hàoma***

Cell phone ***shoujī***

Cell phone number ***shoujī hàoma***

Since its inception in 1997, the cell phone industry has become wildly popular everywhere including far-flung provinces of China. In 1998, as much as 10,000 units have been confiscated by the government from the residents of northern China when it was reported that these units were use as bribe for family and friends. This has eventually led to a big campaign against government corruption.

Proper Way of Making a Phone Call

Confirming if the person at the other end of the line received the call, people say ***"Wéi?"*** (hello). Often this word is uttered in a rising tone on the first consonant by the person on the other end of the call. The reply is the same only that ***"Wéi"*** must be said in a falling tone. Saying ***"Wéi?"*** in a rising tone makes it a question while saying it in a falling tone makes it a statement.

Often the person on the other end will ask ***"Ni nar?"*** (Where are you calling from?) The person does not necessarily ask for the caller's geographical location. Instead, he is asking for the ***dānwèi*** (work unit) the caller belongs to. It is important for them to know this information in order for them to phrase their questions better.

These details will then eventually lead to them asking for the person the call was intended for. As discussed in one of the previous chapters, a person's ***dānwèi*** is important to their life. This determined where a person lives, who and when they can marry and when they can have children. It is customary that the question about ***dānwèi*** is asked over the phone.

Here are a list of things that should be done before, during and after making a phone call:

Pick up the phone. ***náqi diànhuà***

Make a phone call. ***da diànhuà***

Receive a phone call. ***shōudào diànhuà***

Answer a phone call. ***jiē diànhuà***

Return a phone call. ***huí diànhuà***

Leave a message. ***liú yíge huà***

Hang up. *guà diànhuà*

Less Formal Calls

Especially after a long day at work, getting in touch with a ***péngyou*** (friend) or ***tóngshì*** (co-worker) to ***liáotiān*** (chat) is normal. Chinese are very social people. They talk about life and experiences over the phone a lot.

It is not unusual that a ***tóngxué*** (classmate) will call to ask regarding a ***kaoshì*** (exam) the following day or ask your thoughts about a ***wanhuì*** (party) they have been meaning to throw for another ***péngyou*** over the ***zhōumò*** (weekend).

Formal Calls

Making a phone call in places of business are more different than the less formal calls made to a co-worker or friend.

For example, after planning a ***wanhuì***, the next step is to call an ***lhguan*** (hotel) to make a room reservation. For stocks and supplies, phoning a ***shāngdiàn*** (store) to confer about the availability of some desired products for the ***wanhuì***.

Calling a particular ***gōngsī*** (company) trunk line, the operator will ask for the ***fēnjī hàoma*** (extension) of the office desired to be reached. There are times when the extension number is not available in the phone book, the operator can be asked: ***Qingwèn, fēnjī hàoma shì duōshao?*** (May I ask what the extension number is?)

The ***jiēxiànshēng*** (operator) will provide the extension details which can be used as a reference for future calls. Once everything is settled, the ***jiēxiànshēng*** will say: ***"Wo xiànzài jiù gei ni jiē hào."*** (I'll transfer you now.)

There are unfortunate times when despite the call being transferred by the ***jiēxiànshēng***, the line might be busy and ***jiē bù tōng*** (can't connect) and quite possibly even that ***méiyou rén jiē*** (no one answers).

Technical problems like ***diànhuàxiàn duànle*** (the line has been disconnected) persist there's nothing that can be done. This can be ***máfan*** (annoying).

Here are a list of other problems that may be encountered when making a phone call:

No dial tone. ***méiyou bōhàoyīn***

You punched the wrong number. ***ni bōcuò hàomale***

Static ***záyīn***

No one answers méi rén jiē diànhuà

The phone is not working. ***diànhuà huàile***

The line is busy. ***zhànxiàn***

Stay on hold. ***denghòu***

There are times when the telephone line will just ask that a ***you shēng yóujiàn*** (voicemail) is left due to the person sought for is not around or that he is just busy at the moment.

It is different when trying to reach a ***kèhù*** (client) or a ***shēng yì huo bàn*** (business partner) in the regular course of business. Communication technology gave businessmen around the world to establish a good working ***guānxi*** (relationships; connections) with clients and other businessmen. There are times when it is necessary to go through their ***mìshū*** (secretary) before making a scheduling a personal meeting with the person being reached.

The usual instructions provided by most carriers go like this: ***"Nín rúguo shiyòng xuánzhuan bōhào jī, qing bíe guà."*** ("If you have a rotary phone, please stay on the line.") or ***"Nín rúguo shiyòng ànjiàn shì diànhuàjī, qing àn o."*** ("If you have a touchtone phone, please press "o" now.") or further instructions will say: ***"Yào huí dào zhu mùlù qing àn jingzìhào."*** ("If you want to go back to the main menu, please key in the pound sign now.")

Chapter 9. Chinese Grammar Rules

Unlike most other foreign languages, Chinese is easier to learn to speak because it isn't too strict on grammar, sentence constructions, verb tenses and stuff like that. Actually, it does not really need to have the standard "subject+verb" agreement. The verbs, subjects and other parts of the sentence do not have to agree in terms of numbers, tenses and genders.

For example, "He is short" has a subject, verb and an adjective. In Chinese, this is "Ta gao". When translated back to English, it just means "He tall". Chinese adjectives have intrinsic linking verbs. The same is with most other sentences in Chinese. They do not follow the usual grammar rules that most other languages strictly follow.

Learning the basics of Chinese grammar is more for reading and writing, rather than for conversation. Chinese conversations are more forgiving of the sentence structures and grammar. This knowledge and understanding can greatly help when talking in formal settings such as in business or in the academe. Learning grammar is also a step closer to better understanding of the language. It is also a preparation to learning the thousands of Chinese characters, as the rules are better appreciated when writing them.

A word is a word

In other languages, conjugations are very important to convey meaning. In Mandarin Chinese, a word is a word. For example, "go" is used for the pronoun you and I, and plural nouns and pronouns. If the noun or pronoun is singular, the verb form also changes. In this case, it becomes "goes". In Chinese the same word is used for both "go" and "goes", which is qù. For example:

She goes to work. **Tā qù gōngzuò.**

I go to work. **Wǒ qù gōngzuò.**

Aside from the absence of verb conjugations, Chinese language also does not have to change the adjective forms in order to agree with the nouns or pronouns in the sentence.

Topic-based, not subject-based

In most other languages, the subject (doer of the action) is the most important part of the sentence. It is written or spoken of first. In Chinese, they put more importance in the topic of the sentence. For example, look at this sentence:

I don't really like red wine.

This sentence mentions the subject "I" first, which is the subject and is the most important part of the sentence. In Chinese, it is written (and spoken) as:

Hóngjiǔ wǒ bù tài xǐhuan. (Red wine, I don't really like.)

Hóngjiǔ is red wine. This is the topic of the sentence. In Chinese, this is the most important part of the sentence that is why it is written first. Grammar rules in other languages frown upon this type of sentence construction but are very much acceptable in Mandarin.

Another example is this:

Yī zhī bǐ yǒu ma? (A pen- got one?)

Notice that the subject "you" was not even mentioned. This is because the subject is not as important as the topic "pen".

Verb tenses

Learning other languages can get very confusing and difficult because of the verb conjugations to indicate tense. In Mandarin Chinese, time is indicated by a direct referral to time. Using words such as "***zúo tian***" (yesterday), ***jin- tian*** (today), and ***míng tian*** (tomorrow) are deemed enough. There is no need to conjugate the verbs to denote when the action took place.

Chapter 10. Tips to Improve Chinese-Speaking Skills

Getting familiar with a few of the common words and enough phrases can help start small talk and get to know people. The more practice in speaking Chinese, the better you will get at it. Here are a few more tips to help improve your Chinese-speaking skills.

Avoid faking understanding.

Faking understanding what someone said in Chinese is not a good idea. This is the start of a misunderstanding, which can have really bad repercussions. Most people do not want to look stupid but it is a better alternative to pretending to understand and get in trouble later. It is better to admit not able to understand. This will actually help more in learning the language.

Choosing topics is important.

Holding a conversation is not only for practicing learned Chinese words and phrases. It is also a way of learning more about someone, their cultures and ideas. It is also a way to express oneself and teach others something, too. Choose topics that are familiar. Steer clear from politics. It is no use getting into an argument, especially if vocabulary is still limited. Also, it is a good thing to avoid offending people when it comes to differences in political views. No matter where in the world, a simple comment about politics runs a huge risk of offending someone.

Learn to ask questions.

Most often, one would find themselves getting asked about where one came from, hobbies, interests, family, and a few others. Conversations can start to become more of an interview. Ask them back. Learn about the other person. This way, you can also check how to answer questions more naturally and how to pronounce words properly, and how sentences are constructed.

Read body language.

Conversations are not only verbally, but through body language as well. Learn to pay attention to it. Sometimes, people will not say if they understand or if they were offended by what was being said. They may nod or say polite things but then they might suddenly become quieter, talk less, look away more often, or look bewildered. Use body language as a gauge to see if your point is being understood or if you said something wrong.

Communicating with body language

Ever think you know what certain couples are saying or thinking just by observing their gestures and body language? Well, people can make the same observations in China. Although the gestures are different, they contain important clues as to social status between people, their emotions, and so on. Observe Chinese people wherever you can to see if you notice any of the following gestures:

Pointing to one's own nose: You may find this hard to believe, but Chinese people often point to their own noses, often touching them, when they refer to themselves by saying the word "wô" (*waw;* I). The Chinese are probably just as curious as to why Westerners point to their hearts.

Nodding and bowing slightly: When greeting older people, professors, or others in positions of power or prestige, people lower their heads slightly to acknowledge them and show respect. Unlike the Japanese, who bow deeply, the Chinese basically bow with their heads in a slight fashion.

Shaking hands: People of vastly different status generally don't give each other a handshake, but it's common among friends and business colleagues.

Bowing with hands clasped: If you see hand clasping and bowing going on at the same time, you know the participants have something to celebrate. It indicates conveying congratulations or greeting others during special festival occasions. Their hands are held at chest level and their heads are slightly bowed (and they often have big smiles on their faces).

Be attentive for recasting

Recasting means native speakers subtly correct mispronunciations or wrong phrases by repeating the word or phrase in the way it should be spoken. Be mindful of these instances. This is natural, and not meant to be a harsh correction. When native speakers repeat what you have just said, it may be because they were unconsciously or subtly trying to show you the best way to pronounce words.

Practice mental shadowing.

Shadowing means repeating what the other person said in the same way they did. This helps in getting the pronunciation right. Most importantly, it helps in using the different tones in Mandarin Chinese. Do shadowing mentally because doing it aloud can get very awkward.

Chapter 11. The Chengyu

Chengyu are short phrases of Chinese idioms. However, this isn't the same as English idioms. There are thousands of chengyu in the Chinese language. Most people who learn the language strive hard to learn a few of these, too.

Chengyu is typically composed of 4 words strung together. In itself, most chengyu seem to be gibberish. That is unless one knows the entire story behind the chengyu. Speaking Chinese idioms is actually cool. A foreigner who speaks this is deemed impressive, and shows quite a good grasp of the language.

However, chngyu is a minefield. That is, it is easy to use it in the wrong situation. A lot of learners fall into this trap. One can just memorize the 4 words of a Chinese idiom, tell it out loud and look like an expert. Most of the time, learners find out the hard way that these idioms can easily be taken out of context. Does this mean learners should not attempt to learn a few of these idioms? If the goal of learning the language is to gain mastery of it, then these idioms should not be shunned. Instead, embrace a few and slowly expand the knowledge through reading and listening to native speakers how and when they use certain idioms.

A few useful and safe ones include the following:

jiǎo tà shí dì

This literally translates to "to step on solid ground". This idiom means working hard, focusing on the fundamentals and keep at it steadily.

For example:

xiànzài wǒmen yào jìxù jiǎotàshídì. (Right now we need to keep on staying grounded and pushing ahead.)

jiǔ niú yì máo

This literally means “9 cows and 1 strand of cow hair”. Now, this is a classic example of how chengyu can be misused or misunderstood if the meaning is to be taken from the mere words without knowing the story behind it. This idiom is actually referring to something very small in the midst of a much larger situation. It refers to something so small that the effect on the whole may not even be significantly felt.

For example:

diànzǐ shāngwù de yínglì zài zhōngguó zhěngtǐ shāngyè huánjìng zhōng jiǎnzhí shì jiǔniúyìmáo.

Translation: If we consider the Chinese commercial environment in its entirety, E-commerce profits are simply a drop in the bucket.

The phrase “just a drop in the bucket” is one of the closest English idiom that conveys the meaning of jiǔ niú yì máo.

mò míng qí miào

This refers to something so profound, so deep that its real nature and meaning is unfathomable. In simple English, this idiom is used for something of a mysterious nature that is baffling and both difficult to explain and understand.

For example:

tā shuì le jī gōu mò míng qí miào de huà (He said some mysterious words.)

bù kě sī yì

This Chinese idiom is used for something amazing and very unexpected. For example:

zhēn shi bù kě sī yì wǒ de míng zi gēn nǐ yī yàng (It's incredible, I have the same name as you!)

bàn tú ér fèi

This literally means walking down half the road then giving up. It gives a deeper meaning on what can happen when doing something halfway. The story is that doing something halfway can put you in trouble.

A simple example is this:

wǒ búshì bàntúérfèi de rén. (I'm not someone who gives up halfway.)

Conclusion

Thank you again for purchasing this book!

I hope this book was able to help you to learn to speak Chinese fast and easy.

The next step is to start practicing. Moreover, get someone to learn the language with you.

Finally, if you enjoyed this book, please take the time to share your thoughts and post a review on Amazon. We do our best to reach out to readers and provide the best value we can. Your positive review will help us achieve that. It'd be greatly appreciated!

Thank you and good luck!

Check Out My Other Books

Below you'll find some of my other popular books that are popular on Amazon and Kindle as well. Simply click on the links below to check them out. Alternatively, you can visit my author page on Amazon to see other work done by me.

The Best of England For Tourists

http://amzn.to/1rv7RVZ

The Best of Brazil For Tourists

http://amzn.to/1sCoSdT

The Best of Beautiful Greece For Tourists

http://amzn.to/1u9Xclw

The Best of Spain For Tourists

http://amzn.to/1zHGGII

The Best of Beautiful Germany For Tourists

http://amzn.to/V4SoiT

The Best of Beautiful France For Tourists

http://amzn.to/1yD7yal

The Best of Beautiful Netherlands For Tourists

http://amzn.to/1oU2hKF

The Best of Italy For Tourists

http://amzn.to/1kNIqYm

Portuguese for Beginners

http://amzn.to/1qgRyKH

Greek for Beginners

http://amzn.to/1u385SO

German for Beginners

http://amzn.to/Y3JxOV

French for Beginners

http://amzn.to/1CgsxVc

Dutch for Beginners

http://amzn.to/1pZhdb3

English for Beginners

http://amzn.to/1qZbmCz

Italian for Beginners

http://amzn.to/1pxjRFL

Spanish for Beginners

http://amzn.to/1lDoJFr

The Best Of Canada For Tourists

http://amzn.to/1uLV9QW

Travel Box Set #1 The Best of Brazil For Tourists & Portuguese for Beginners

http://amzn.to/WoFSzA

Travel Box Set #2 The Best of England For Tourists & English for Beginners

http://amzn.to/Y3M2kv

Travel Box Set #3 The Best of Beautiful France For Tourists & French for Beginners

http://amzn.to/1CgvogX

Travel Box Set #4 The Best of Beautiful Germany For Tourists & German for Beginners

http://amzn.to/1qgUF5y

Travel Box Set #5 The Best of Beautiful Greece For Tourists & Greek for Beginners

http://amzn.to/1phepk9

If the links do not work, for whatever reason, you can simply search for these titles on the Amazon website to find them.

32174945R00042

Made in the USA
Middletown, DE
04 January 2019